Dearly, Nearly, Insincerely

What Is an Adverb?

Adverb: A word that describes when, how, where, how often, and how much.

Dearly, Nearly, Insincerely

What Is an Adverb?

by Brian P. Cleary

illustrated by Brian Gable

CAROLRHODA BOOKS, INC. / MINNEAPOLIS

Adverbs tell us when and how,

Like, quickly do your homework, now.

They often help describe the verbs,

Like, **patiently** plant peas and herbs.

PEAS

Frankly, this hot dog just couldn't be better.

Sheepishly, Fred found he'd ruined his sweater.

If they tell us **how**, they're an "adVerb of manner,"

Like, slowly this summer, my sister got tanner.

Or, quietly sneak up to
where she is sunning

And give her a squirt from
the hose that is running.

Always eat cookies, and never eat pine.

Sometimes I'm nervous, but usually fine.

Or Johnny is somewhat afraid of the spider,

And Mickey has **hardly** been touching his cider.

First, I was tired,

 then, I was woozy,

Next, I began feeling sleepy and snoozy.

They modify **adverbs,** like, she sang **quite** nicely.

Or he speaks so **swiftly** but **very** precisely.

Presently, pleasantly, properly praise.

Speedily, sometimes quite greedily, graze.

Bitterly angry, bitingly cold,

Brilliantly burgundy, Shockingly old.

That Well's how you felt, and good was your day.

Yes, **Well** is a **very** deep Subject, I'd Say!

Dearly, nearly, insincerely,

Daily, weekly, monthly, yearly,

Truly, deeply, sadly, badly—

I tell you these are adverbs, gladly.

And so are
sleekly and
uniquely,

Bravely,
boldly,

coldly, meekly.

Brightly, slightly, impolitely—

You'd say that these
are **adverbs, rightly**.

So, what is an **adVerb?**

Do you know?

ABOUT THE AUTHOR & ILLUSTRATOR

BRIAN P. CLEARY is the author of several other picture books, including A Mink, a Fink, a Skating Rink: What Is a Noun?, To Root, to Toot, to Parachute: What Is a Verb?, Hairy, Scary, Ordinary: What Is an Adjective?, Under, Over, By the Clover: What Is a Preposition?, and Rainbow Soup: Adventures in Poetry.

BRIAN GABLE is the illustrator of Under, Over, By the Clover: What Is a Preposition? He lives in Toronto, Ontario, where he works as a political cartoonist.

Carolrhoda Books, Inc., a division of Lerner Publishing Group
241 First Avenue North, Minneapolis, MN 55401 U.S.A.

Website address: www.lernerbooks.com

Library of Congress Cataloging-in-Publication Data

Cleary, Brian P., 1959—
    Dearly, nearly, insincerely : what is an adverb? / by Brian P. Cleary;
    illustrated by Brian Gable.
        p.   cm. — (Words are categorical)
    Summary: Rhyming text and illustrations present numerous examples of
adverbs and their functions.
    ISBN: 1—57505—807—3 (lib. bdg. : alk. paper)
    1. English language—Adverb—Juvenile literature. [1. English language—
Adverb.] I. Gable, Brian, 1949— II. Title.
PE1325 .C57 2003
428.2—dc21   2002003012

Manufactured in the United States of America
1 2 3 4 5 6 7 — JR — 09 08 07 06 05 04